WELLS CATHEDRAL

Contents

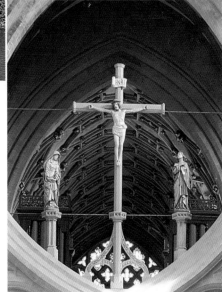

Above:
The Cathedral seen from the moat of the Bishop's Palace.

Right:
The Rood, designed by Sir Charles Nicholson in 1924, is set at the crossing where the medieval figures stood.

History Chart

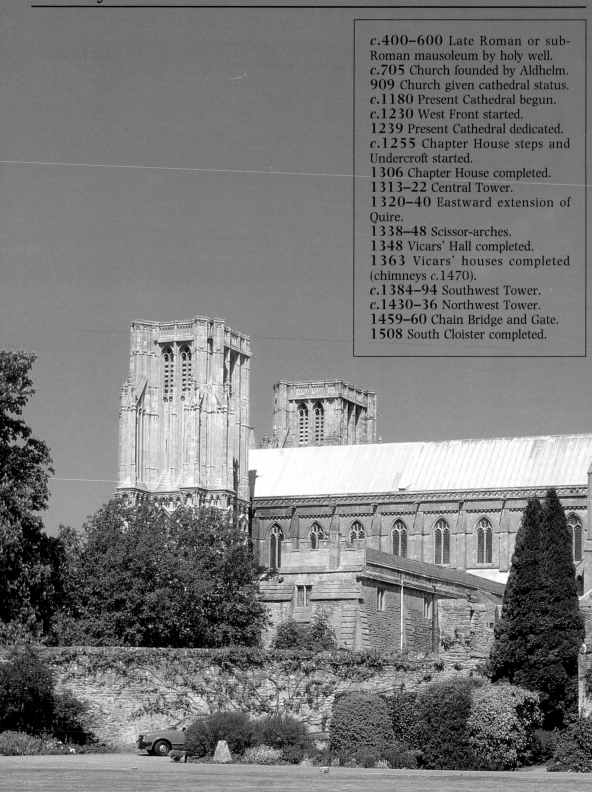

*c.*400–600 Late Roman or sub-Roman mausoleum by holy well.
*c.*705 Church founded by Aldhelm.
909 Church given cathedral status.
*c.*1180 Present Cathedral begun.
*c.*1230 West Front started.
1239 Present Cathedral dedicated.
*c.*1255 Chapter House steps and Undercroft started.
1306 Chapter House completed.
1313–22 Central Tower.
1320–40 Eastward extension of Quire.
1338–48 Scissor-arches.
1348 Vicars' Hall completed.
1363 Vicars' houses completed (chimneys *c.*1470).
*c.*1384–94 Southwest Tower.
*c.*1430–36 Northwest Tower.
1459–60 Chain Bridge and Gate.
1508 South Cloister completed.

The Dean's Message

Our Cathedral is a living community, drawing upon a rich inheritance of history, faith and beauty. It is a jewel in the crown of English Cathedrals, and a working building. Its chief work is worship. From its beginning the worship of Almighty God has been offered here, and is offered still day after day. The Cathedral is also host to the celebration of great events in the life of the wider church and nation, as well as the natural place to be for quieter, more reflective or sadder moments. If you come as a visitor, we hope that you will leave as a pilgrim. Few remain unmoved by the majesty of this sermon in stone. Ask not only what and when; ask also why.

Richard Lewis
DEAN OF WELLS

Saxon Beginnings

Three springs close to the Bishop's Palace give Wells its name. They were probably associated with a shrine of some sort long before Christianity came. Excavations in the Camery, on the south side of the Cathedral, in 1894 and 1978–80 revealed foundations of late Roman and Saxon burial places, and evidence of the chapels and minster church which grew from these beginnings. This church extended diagonally under the present Palm Churchyard to the market place, near Penniless Porch. It is thought that the market place and main streets of Wells were deliberately aligned upon this great Saxon church, just as the church and its associated chapels were aligned upon the holy wells.

This was the church named for St Andrew, which Aldhelm, Bishop of Sherborne, founded in 705, perhaps under the patronage of King Ina of Wessex whose modern memorial tablet lies in the nave of the present Cathedral. When the Diocese of Wells was created in 909, with its own bishop, Aldhelm's church became the first Cathedral Church of St Andrew.

After Bishop Giso died in 1088, his successor John of Tours moved the see to Bath. The old church in Wells was disdained, and its associated buildings destroyed. This situation stirred Bishop Robert of Lewes (1136–66) to restore and enlarge the decayed church. He gave it a Dean and Canons to be responsible under him for its life and work, as the Dean and Canons are responsible for the Cathedral today.

The Saxon font has survived from the first Cathedral and is the oldest object in the present building, signifying the continuity of Christian life between the old church and the new, through Baptism from which that life stems. The font was originally decorated with carvings of saints, standing under rounded arches. Traces of their haloes can still be seen. At some time the figures were chipped off and the arches reshaped so that the font might better match its new setting. The font is still used for baptisms, as it has been for over one thousand years.

The New Cathedral and the Quire

Left: (13) (15)
The Quire looking east, with the retroquire and Lady Chapel beyond, and the great Jesse window c.1340 high above.

Below: (1)
The elaborate north porch is the main entrance to the Cathedral.

Below, right: (13)
Misericord (on show in the retroquire) of a man killing a wyvern, c.1330. Secular subjects in lively detail are characteristic of these hidden carvings.

Bishop Robert's successor Reginald de Bohun, Bishop of Bath 1174–91, determined to give the Dean and Canons a new church in which to work and worship. He started to construct the present building on a fresh site north of the old Cathedral. This explains why the present Cathedral has no grand entrance from the city, but is 'off-set' from the market place, behind narrow gates.

As the *cathedra* or bishop's throne was still at Bath Abbey, the new church lacked cathedral status, but it was nevertheless planned on an ambitious scale. Work began in 1179–80 with the Quire, which was, as it still is, the centre of daily worship.

From the start, the building was planned all of a piece in the English 'Gothic', an innovation in architectural style antedating the great Gothic cathedrals of Lincoln and Bourges by at least

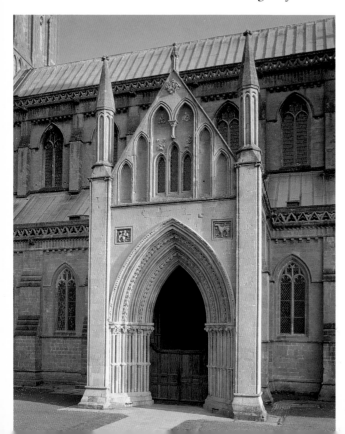

five years. Work progressed from the Quire westwards down the Nave. Halfway along the Nave, on the north side, is the main entrance, with its high and elaborately decorated porch. It made a fitting entrance for the Dean and principal dignitaries, who lived in the Liberty or precinct on that side of the Cathedral. The church was dedicated in 1239, though work on details continued until about 1260. From start to finish, realisation of the grand design had taken about eighty years.

A cathedral, however, is never finished. It continues to grow and develop, and this is reflected in its building history. About 1320 work was begun to extend the Quire eastwards, joining it with the eastern Lady Chapel. The different style of the three eastern bays of the present Quire clearly marks this extension. Work progressed slowly, interrupted by other building projects, and was not finished until about 1340.

An organ has stood above the entrance to the Quire since about 1335. The present instrument was built by Henry Willis in 1857, rebuilt and enlarged in 1909/10, and again in 1973/4. The organ case was completed in 1974.

The wooden stalls in the Quire were made c.1330–40. Under each hinged seat is a misericord, a wooden carving which supports a small ledge – a discreet prop for clerics standing through long services. Three of these carvings are to be seen in the retroquire. The back stalls with their elaborate stone canopies were constructed for the Canons in 1848.

Right:
North Quire clerestory window of *c*.1345. St George, patron saint of England, and St Leo, Pope 440–61, rich in details of medieval armour and vestments.

The rich hues of the modern embroideries in the Quire complement those of the windows above. The great east window *c*.1340, known also as the Golden Window from its glowing colours, shows Christ's kinship with King David, son of Jesse. It is among the oldest and finest of Jesse windows in this country. On either side are two windows depicting saints; all four are *c*.1345.

There is more medieval glass in the windows of the Quire Aisles. These well-lit processional ways developed as worship became increasingly elaborate in the 13th century. They lead round the Quire to the retroquire, chapels and Lady Chapel at the eastern end. Among the tombs and memorials are effigies of the Saxon Bishops of Wells, made about 1200 when their bones were brought from the old Cathedral. This was part of the campaign to regain cathedral status for Wells, showing that there had been Saxon bishops here whose memory was revered still in the new church. The campaign was successful. In 1244/5, soon after the dedication of the new church, the Pope decreed that the Bishop should be Bishop of 'Bath and Wells'; thus Wells became a cathedral once more. Bath Abbey was dissolved along with all other religious houses in 1539; Wells Cathedral, always a cathedral of secular canons and never a monastery, survived.

Right: ⑨ ⑭
South Quire Aisle, looking east towards St John the Baptist's Chapel, leading to the retroquire and Lady Chapel. Beyond tombs including those of a Saxon bishop and Bishop Lord Arthur Hervey (1894), are the fine iron railings of 1450 around the chantry chapel and tomb of Bishop Bekynton.

The Chapter House

Left:
The graceful stairway, worn by many feet, turns into the Chapter House. The window at the top of the stair was cut through in 1459, to take the narrower stairs up and over the Chain Bridge to the Vicars' Hall.

Right:
The Chapter House, its vaulted roof of 32 ribs supported by a central pillar. The Chapter stalls, each with its nameplate, line the walls.

Below:
Heads carved between arches of the Chapter House stalls range from king to peasant, and from solemn to humorous. Here a king and a bearded patriarch contrast with a puckish man in a medieval bonnet.

The restoration of Wells to cathedral status marked a new stage in the organisation and independence of the Dean and Canons, known collectively as the Chapter. As the Quire is their principal place of worship, so the Chapter House, begun about 1250, was built to be their place of business.

The difficulty of providing a spacious, well-lit room was dramatically solved. A narrow medieval doorway opens onto the processional staircase, curving up to the first-floor Chapter House. The staircase windows contain the oldest stained glass in the Cathedral, c.1290. The octagonal Chapter House itself was finished in 1306. Its huge windows have lost most of their original glass, but a few Resurrection scenes survive in tracery lights. Around the walls are the seats for the members of the Chapter.

Today, the full Chapter meets on special occasions. Day-to-day affairs are in the hands of the five Dignitaries – the Dean, the Precentor, the Archdeacon of Wells, the Chancellor and the Treasurer, as established by Bishop Robert in the 12th century. The Dean is Chairman of the Chapter, vigilant in every aspect of Cathedral life. The Precentor has charge of the music; the Organist and Choir are directly responsible to him. The Archdeacon of Wells is an important link between Cathedral and Diocese. The Chancellor, originally Chapter secretary, is responsible still for the Cathedral's archives and Library. Part of his duty is to promote theological study. The Treasurer is the guardian of the Cathedral's furnishings, vestments and plate, responsible through his team of Virgers for ensuring that the Cathedral remains a place fit for worship. These five dignitaries constitute the Administrative Chapter, responsible together for the Cathedral; whilst month by month each undertakes in turn a particular responsibility as Canon in Residence.

Left and **inset:**
The polygonal Lady
Chapel, completed by
1326, with detail of the
east window *c.*1320.
Angels swinging censers
look upwards to Christ in
Majesty at the top.

Every medieval cathedral had its Lady Chapel, built in honour of the Mother of Jesus. She has been revered in the Church from the beginning, but this devotion increased in intensity during the 13th and 14th centuries. Our Lady Chapels – Wells had two of them for centuries – are an indication of this.

The present octagonal Lady Chapel, completed in 1326, was built as a separate structure. It was, however, precisely aligned with the Quire, and the intricate mathematics of its design have only recently become clear. The retroquire, a graceful forest of pillars, was subsequently built to join the Lady Chapel to the main building.

The upper parts of the Lady Chapel windows and the tracery contain the original glass of *c.*1320–26, although much of the rest is a brilliant jumble of fragments salvaged from this and other parts of the Cathedral. These windows emphasise how much medieval beauty was destroyed, notably in the Civil War (1642–47) and Monmouth's Rebellion (1685). The main lights of the east window were restored in 1845 by T. H. Willement, who also designed and executed the painting on the roof vault.

Left:
The intricate star-burst of the ribs in the medieval roof vault of the Lady Chapel sets off T. H. Willement's delicate decoration.

Overleaf:
Aerial view of Wells Cathedral from the north-west, with the moated Bishop's Palace beyond.

The Nave and the West Front

The Nave gives visitors their first impression of the Cathedral interior. The lines of pillars, the triforium and high vault above, draw the eye irresistibly eastward to the crossing with scissor-arches, Rood and Quire screen.

Work on the Nave started at the crossing, but ceased for a time when the Pope, in 1208, closed all churches in the kingdom because of his quarrel with King John. When work resumed, the overall design continued unaltered to the west end, but the sharp eye will detect a 'break', marked by a change from small to large building stones, and from restrained to luxuriant foliage on capitals, among other details. The decoration of the high vaults, though restored in 1844 and again in 1985, follows the medieval pattern.

High up at the west end of the Nave, on the north side, is the bearded head of a man wearing a mason's cap. This may portray Adam Lock, master mason, architect of this part of the Cathedral. He died in 1229, ten years before the Nave was completed. His successor Thomas Norreys finished it, and undertook the decoration of the West Front, between about 1230 and 1250.

Like an elaborate altar screen, the array of statuary on the West Front spreads across the breadth of the Nave and the towers on either side, continuing round Bubwith's tower. Kings and knights, saints and angels, scenes from Old Testament and New lead the eye upward through the intricate band of Resurrection figures and the row of Apostles, to the Risen Christ. Flanked by six-winged seraphim, this figure was put up in 1985 to replace what remained of the medieval original. Traces of paint found during the 1980s restoration show that the statues and mouldings were originally brightly coloured, making an impact which would be startling to modern eyes.

Such an array of medieval sculpture is a song of praise in stone, a great procession worshipping God and expressing for Christ's servants in all ages the hope of eternal life in him. Colourful as the statues above, worshippers assembled on Cathedral Green to pass beneath the stone multitude into the Nave.

The Nave and its aisles were designed as a great space to accommodate such processions. Stone benches around the walls for the infirm were the only seating in the medieval Nave. Today the Nave is a place of worship, as it never was in the Middle Ages. When there are many communicants, the Sunday Sung Eucharist is held here. Also it is frequently the setting for special events drawing hundreds of people.

Right:
The Nave, from the west end looking east to the Rood and the great 'scissor-arches' at the crossing.

Left:
Carvings round a capital in the South Transept tell a story: A man and a boy are stealing fruit, probably grapes. The man holds a pruning knife, the boy holds the basket of fruit. Both look around guiltily…as a farm hand with an axe points them out to the farmer. He, armed with a pitchfork, sets off…to catch them. He hits the thief over the head. Such incidents must have been common enough in the vineyards which existed in this area in the 1200s.

The Central Tower

The central tower, originally the bell tower, was built in two stages. The first finished about the level of the nave roof. In 1313 Dean John Godelee, ambitious to enhance the Cathedral further, added another more elaborate stage topped with a spire. The result was near disaster. In 1338 the tower began to lean and crack because the foundations failed to support the additional height and weight.

The spectacular solution of William Joy, master mason, was to construct during the ten years 1338–48 a scissor-arch on three sides of the crossing under the tower. Supplemented by hidden buttresses, these scissor-arches redistributed the stresses and braced the tower. This dramatic feat of engineering proved a triumphant success. The central tower remains stable to this day. Its bells were removed to the southwest tower, built c.1384 to accommodate them. Its upper stage was reconstructed, without a spire, after a fire in 1438/9.

Left, below:
Tiny figures crowd a quatrefoil on the West Front, as they listen to Christ expound the Scriptures in the synagogue at Nazareth.

Left, above:
High on the northwest tower of the West Front a knight in chain-mail stares out over Wells. The fine detail of his eyes peering through his barrel helm can never have been seen from the ground far below.

Left:
An exuberant design of a lizard eating berries, expertly carved on a 14th-century corbel in the North Transept.

Right:
The scissor-arches of the crossing, looking into the South Transept towards the font.

Wells, a secular cathedral and never a monastery, nonetheless has a cloister. It encloses the Palm Churchyard, the Cathedral dignitaries' burying ground, where the 'dipping place' leads down into Bishop Bekynton's conduit.

The East Cloister has always been the Bishop's entrance to his Cathedral. Its graceful Early English doorway is one of the few survivals from the original, narrow 13th-century cloisters, which underwent a major reconstruction in the 15th century. The Cathedral, as a centre of learning with its own school, acquired many books, and by the 1400s needed a proper library to house them. Bishop Bubwith, who died in 1424, left 1,000 marks (nearly £^{1}/$_4$ million in modern currency) to build a library over the East Cloister.

The Library is one of the longest of its date in England. Its many small windows, like those of the matching Choir School built by Bishop Bekynton above the West Cloister *c.*1460, are characteristic of medieval schools and libraries. The Library contains about 6,000 books, mainly of the 16th–18th centuries, some

Above:
This Psalter was made for Hailes Abbey in Gloucestershire by the Flemish scribe and illuminator Peter Meghen (known as Peter the One-eyed) in 1514.

still chained to the book presses which, with their desks, were fitted *c.*1685 at a cost of more than £300.

The books, mostly gifts of Bishops, Deans and Canons, disclose the interests of Cathedral dignitaries of the time: not only theology, but also law, medicine, travel, languages, botany, mathematics. The Library also contains archives of the Dean and Chapter, from the 10th century to the present.

Right:
The medieval Cathedral Library, refurnished with pine book presses and desks in 1685. The many 15th-century windows were designed to give maximum light. The 13th-century corbel head is one of a number reused to support the roof.

Left:
Looking south through the 15th-century East Cloister to the 13th-century doorway of the original and obviously narrower cloister.

The Clock, a Chantry and the Chain Gate

Thomas Bekynton, Bishop of Bath and Wells 1443–65, Lord Privy Seal and secretary to King Henry VI, left the Cathedral and the city of Wells everlastingly in his debt. Having built the Choir School over the West Cloister, he showed his fatherly concern for the choristers in the detailed rules he made for their health and education.

He cared equally for the men of his Cathedral Choir, the Vicars Choral. In 1459 he built the Chain Bridge over what was then the main Bath road, linking the Vicars' Hall and the Chapter House stair, so that the Vicars could come and go without crossing a busy street. The Chain Gate beneath may have been closed occasionally with chains, hence its name. Bekynton also left money to improve the houses in Vicars' Close.

For the townspeople at his palace gate he built the row of twelve houses in the Market Place still known as The New Works, supplying them with clean water from St Andrew's Well, which still flows down the High Street. The City Council, in accordance with the terms of

Above: (14)
The contrasting effigies of worldly magnificence and earthly decay, on Bishop Thomas Bekynton's tomb (1450), are a reminder of what all must come to.

Left: (16)
The Chain Bridge, 1459, clearly links the Vicars' Hall (on the left) to the Cathedral (on the right).

Right, above:
The external clock, built to face the Canons' houses on Cathedral Green.

Right: (4)
The intricately painted clock in the North Transept, the oldest cathedral clock-face in Britain, with the carved Christus (1956) below.

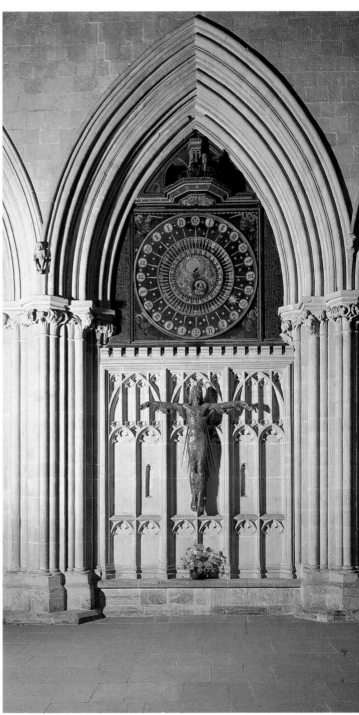

Bekynton's grant of water, come yearly on the anniversary of his death, to commemorate him in his chantry chapel.

Chantries were endowed by the rich and powerful so that mass might be offered daily for them and their kin after death. Three chantry chapels survive here. Two elaborate chapels in the Nave were founded *c.*1424 and *c.*1489, to commemorate Bishop Nicholas Bubwith and Hugh Sugar, Treasurer and one of Bekynton's executors. Bekynton's own magnificent chantry chapel, built fifteen years before his death, survives in all its colourful splendour. It is dominated by his double effigy, in full pontificals above and as a cadaver below.

The proliferation of services at the many altars in the Cathedral made precise time-keeping essential. To achieve this a clock, first mentioned in 1392, was installed. It still keeps time today. One elaborate clockface inside has the tournament above and the quarterjack Jack Blandiver nearby; the other, outside, is set below two medieval warriors who smite a bell.

The Vicars Choral and Vicars' Close

Vicars Choral have been an integral part of Cathedral life since the 12th century. Who they are and what they do will be understood by realising that *vicar* means *deputy*. Canons, not bound to the Cathedral as monks to a monastery, appointed deputies (vicars) to undertake duties which they themselves could not or would not perform. Then, as now, music was central to Cathedral worship, and vicars were chosen for skill in singing – hence Vicars Choral.

In 1348 Bishop Ralph of Shrewsbury formed them into a community or college, and drew up for them a code of rules. He built Vicars' Close to house them, and Vicars' Hall where they ate together and transacted business.

Vicars' Close consisted of 42 small houses in two rows with the chapel at the far end. Religious upheavals in the 16th century reduced the number of Vicars Choral, but they were now free to marry. Houses were put together into larger dwellings, to accommodate their families. Gardens added in front gave the appearance of a medieval street.

Through all these changes, the work of the Vicars Choral continued as it does today. Members of the College of Vicars Choral – the gentlemen of the choir – still live in Vicars' Close, as do other members of the Cathedral foundation. Along with the choristers, the Vicars Choral sing daily in the Cathedral, and form with their families an important part of the Cathedral community.

The Cathedral has had an organ since the early 1300s. The Organist is also Master of the Choristers and, under the

Right: (16) (17)
The Vicars' Hall and entrance to Vicars' Close, with the Chain Bridge to the Cathedral.

Far right: (18)
Vicars' Close, built by 1363 and improved *c.*1465, retains the features of a medieval college. Later adaptations have not destroyed its atmosphere. The Vicars' chapel, built by Bishop Bubwith, stands at the far end.

Right: (17)
Vicars' Hall, completed 1348, contains fine 17th-century panelling and furniture.

Precentor's direction, responsible for the Cathedral's musical life. Appropriately, he too how lives in Vicars' Close.

Four houses in Vicars' Close are used by the Cathedral School, an amalgamation of the Cathedral's medieval Choir School and Grammar School. It provides for boys and girls of all ages, and is famous for its music school. It occupies many of the historic houses in The Liberty.

The Cathedral Today

Left: ⑮
The throne or *cathedra*, from which the word 'cathedral' derives, is the Bishop's seat in the Quire. Throne and stalls are hung with richly coloured embroideries, made 1937–49.

Below:
Choristers and Vicars Choral grouped together on the Chapter House stairway.

The Cathedral has become increasingly a tourist attraction, although it remains above all a place of prayer. In a very different world it still fulfils the functions for which it was built. Daily, the Dean and Chapter, Vicars Choral and choristers, with worshippers from far and near, come together to praise God, to pray for the Bishop and his diocese, and with them for people everywhere.

Skilled volunteers welcome visitors and introduce them to the building. The Cathedral Shop and Cloisters Restaurant flourish in meeting their needs. Four permanent Virgers, named for the *virges* or silver rods which they carry in processions, are responsible for good order and cleanliness in the Cathedral, and for all arrangements both for daily services and special events. Expert administra-tive support is provided by the Cathedral Secretary and his staff. Maintaining the Cathedral are the Clerk of the Works, the Master Mason and their men, usually at work somewhere around the building.

There are some 3,000 Friends of Wells Cathedral, from all over the world. They express their love for the Cathedral by financing such projects as the restoration of the Cloisters and of the Chapter House. The figure of Christ (1985) at the apex of the West Front is their thank-offering for their Golden Jubilee.

The Cathedral is a busy place, and rightly so; but it strives to preserve an atmosphere of peace and serenity, drawing us to wait upon God and to renew our strength in him.